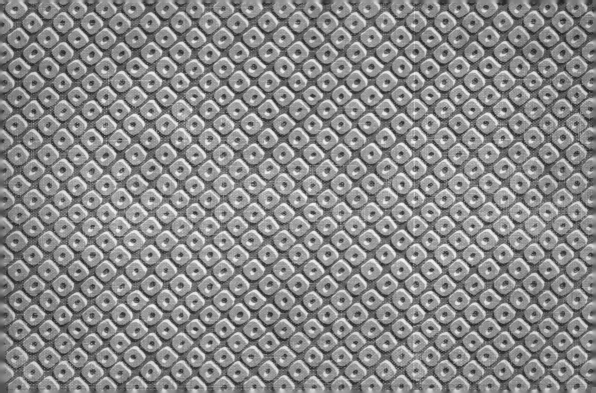

Published by Hallmark Gift Books,
a division of Hallmark Cards, Inc.,
Kansas City, MO 64141
Visit us on the Web at Hallmark.com.

Editorial Director: Delia Berrigan
Editor: Kim Schworm Acosta
Art Director: Chris Opheim
Designer: Brian Pilachowski
Production Designer: Dan Horton
Contributing Writers: Renee Daniels, Jake
Gahr, Bill Gray, Keion Jackson, Matt Gowen,
Katherine Stano

ISBN: 978-1-63059-9-133
BOK1053

Made in China
0917

GOOD GRIEF!

Hallmark

EANUTS PICK-ME-UPS

OR WHEN YOU NEED 'EM MOST

ERSPECTIVE IS EVERYTHING.

GO AHEAD.
LET IT OUT.

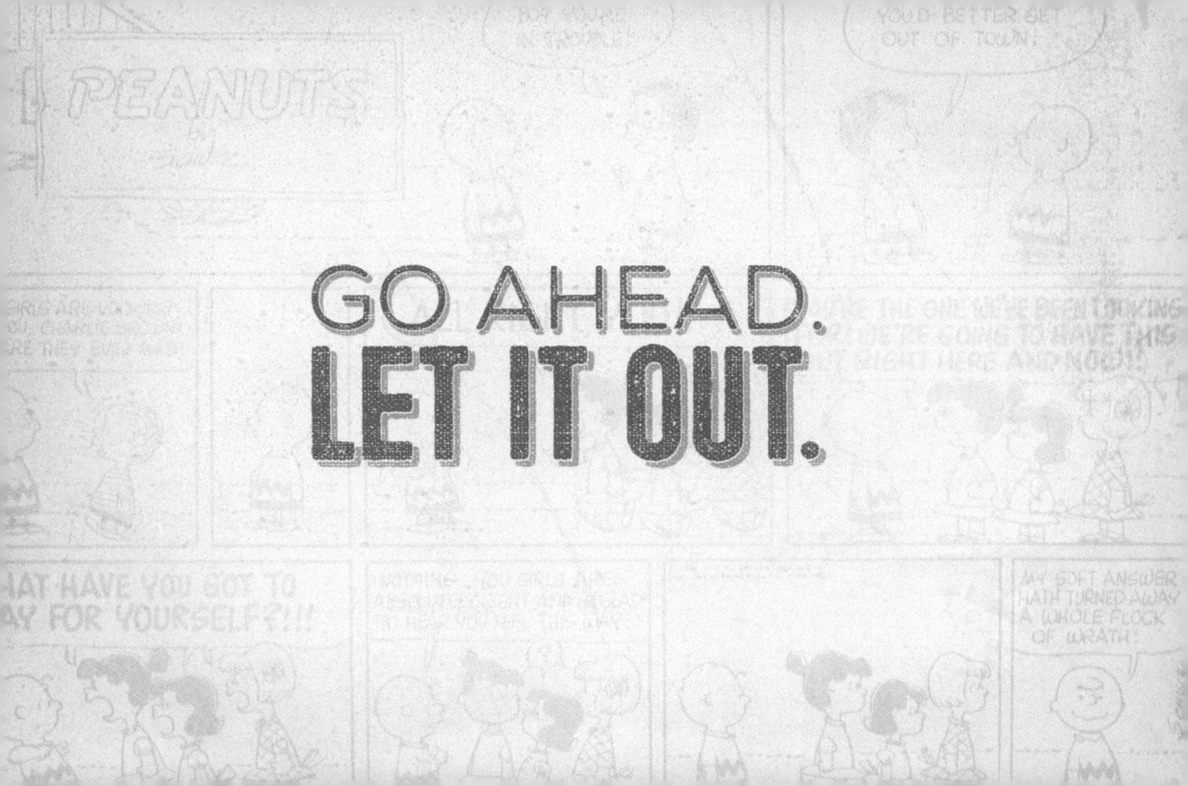

BE YOUR
OWN
HERO.

DO WHAT MAKES YOU
FEEL CARED FOR.

3-2

OME DAYS IT JUST FINDS YOU, **NO MATTER WHAT.**

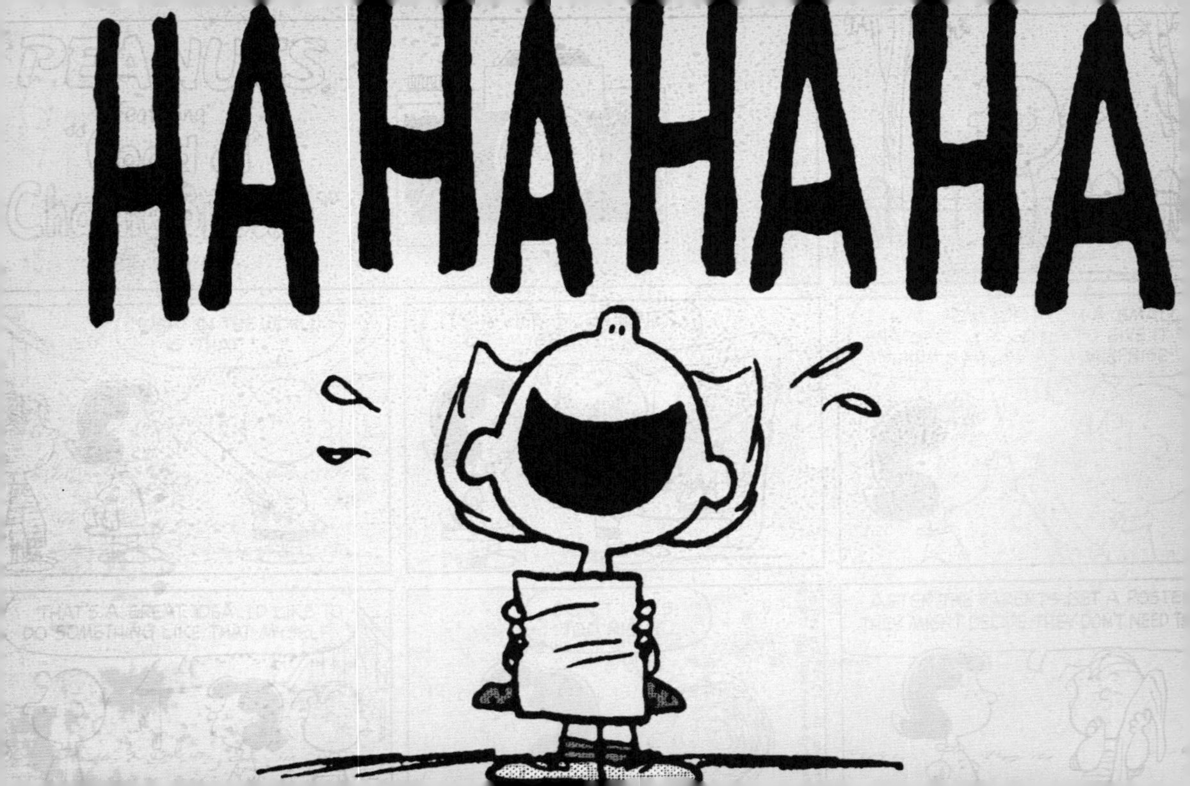
HAHAHAHA

LAUGH IN THE FACE OF . . .
EVERYTHING.

PEANUTS
featuring
"Good ol' Charlie Brown"
SOONER OR LATER,
GOOD THINGS
ALWAYS
COME AROUND.

SOME DAYS ARE "SINK INTO TH

METHING YOU LOVE.

WHAT DOESN'T
KNOCK YOU OUT COLD
ONLY MAKES YOU
STRONGER.

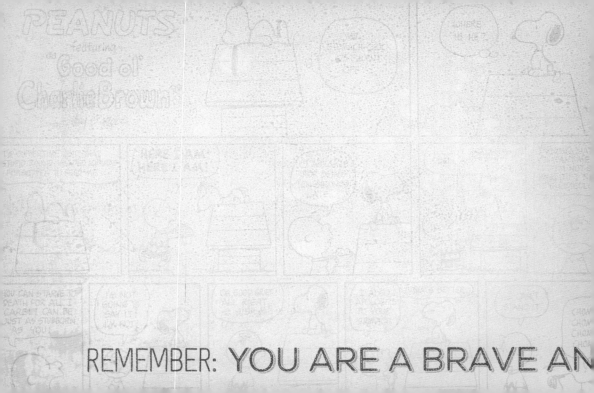

REMEMBER: YOU ARE A BRAVE AN

IF YOU KICK Y

NOTHING CA

R FEET UP, KEEP YOU DOWN.

CERTAIN THINGS
JUST CAN'T BE AVOIDED.

PEANUTS
featuring
"Good ol' Charlie Brown"
SOME DAYS, YA GOTTA LET S

EONE ELSE RISE AND SHINE.

TAKING TIME TO COOL OFF
IS **ALWAYS A GOOD IDEA.**

"SOMETIMES WE ALL NEED A LITTLE PAMPERING TO HELP US FEEL BETTER."
—LINUS

IF IT'S GOING **TO BE A BAD DAY,** YOU MIGHT AS WELL **MAKE IT INTERESTING.**

"THERE ARE GOOD PEOPLE. THE
THERE ARE MEDIU
THIS IS THE WAY IT HA

THIS IS PROBABL

IF YOU NEED A HUG,
DON'T BE AFRAID
TO ASK FOR IT.

EVERYBODY HAS THOSE
"DIDN'T *SEE THAT* COMING"
MOMENTS.

MESSINESS HAPPENS.

...HAT MATTERS.
IT'S THE GETTING UP.

IF YOU HAVE ENJOYED THIS BOOK
OR IT HAS TOUCHED YOUR LIFE IN SOME WAY,
WE WOULD LOVE TO HEAR FROM YOU.

PLEASE SEND YOUR COMMENTS TO:
HALLMARK BOOK FEEDBACK
P.O. BOX 419034
MAIL DROP 100
KANSAS CITY, MO 64141

OR E-MAIL US AT:
BOOKNOTES@HALLMARK.COM

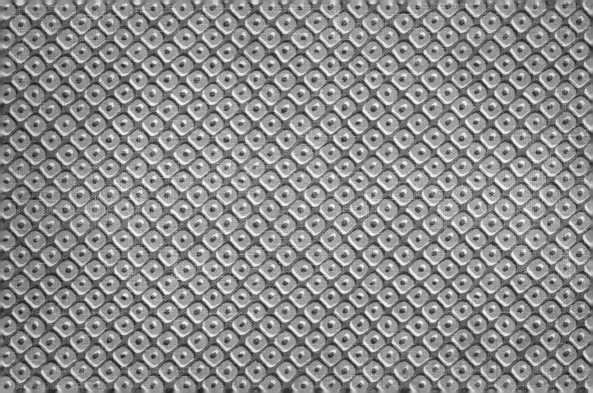

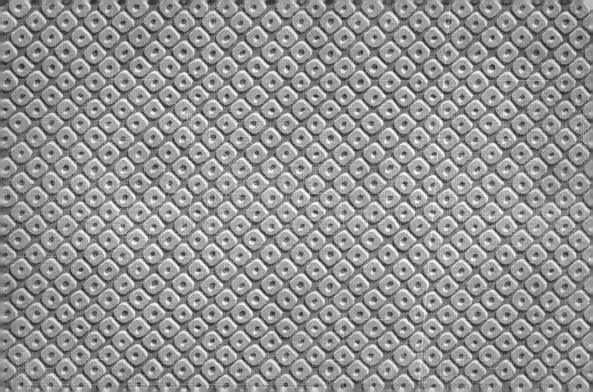